When I Cook, They Run

The Art of Miserable Meal Making

Recipes and advice that will have them running from your table!

By Karen Kallet

Twenty12 Publishing

Phoenix, Arizona

When I Cook, They Run – The Art of Miserable Meal Making
By Karen Kallet

Published by:
Twenty12 Publishing
PO Box 26756
Phoenix, Arizona 85068-6756, USA
Telephone: 602-866-0342 Fax: 602-866-7421
You can reach the author with your comments at:
e-mail: kallet@ix.netcom.com

This book is available by mail from the publisher for $14.95 plus $4.00 shipping, plus Arizona sales tax, if applicable. But try your book store first!

Cover illustration: Frank Ybarra, Artist/Illustrator
Cover design: Bob & Eileen Burick, Burick Communications Design, Inc.
Author photo: Jeff Noble, Noble Studios
Editor: Karla Olson, Via Press
Interior Design: Lisa Liddy, The Printed Page

First edition, First Printing: February, 1998
Library of Congress Catalog Card Number: 97-91071
ISBN: 1-891512-92-7

Publisher's Cataloging-in-Publication
(Provided by Quality Books, Inc.)

Kallet, Karen.
When I cook, they run : the art of miserable meal making: recipes and advice that will have them running from your table! / by Karen Kallet—1st ed.
p. cm.
Includes index.
Preassigned LCCN: 97-91071
ISBN : 1-891512-92-7

1. Cookery—Humor. 2. American wit and humor. I. Title.

PN6231.C624K35 1998 641.5'0207
QBI97-41353

Printed in the United States of America
10 9 8 7 6 5 4 3 2 1

Dedication

This cookbook has taken me over ten years to complete. I hope you have as much fun reading it as I have had creating it.

It is dedicated to my husband, who first encouraged me to make this cookbook more than just a dream. He wanted me to put into words what he has been experiencing for years.

There are so many other people to thank. To Rich, who lent me my first word processor. To Cathy, Suzanne and Pat, who encouraged me to reach my goal. To Jennifer, whose support made it possible to complete this cookbook. To Eileen and Bob, who rescued me when I needed a cover design. To Frank, whose illustration talent was so kindly given.

To my mother, grandmother and aunt, whose cooking was, and still is, way too good. To my sons, who never really liked my cooking, even when I tried. I dedicate this cookbook to all of you, for through you was born The Art of Miserable Meal Making.

When I Cook, They Run
Disclaimer

The purpose of this cookbook is for entertainment and education only. The recipes and ideas in this cookbook are never to be used to harm yourself, your family or your guests in any way. So don't do anything stupid. Everything in this cookbook is edible. There are no dog hairs or spoiled food, so don't get any ideas of the sort.

The author and Twenty12 Publishing shall have neither liability, nor responsibility to any person or entity with respect to any loss or damage caused, or alleged to be caused, directly or indirectly by the information contained in this cookbook.

Persons using this cookbook and engaging in the activities therein accept the responsibility for their own actions and to monitor such activities as to not cause any harm. The publisher and author assume no liability by any accident, injury or mishap that may arise from the recipes and activities detailed in this cookbook.

Every effort has been made to make this cookbook as complete as possible. However, there may be mistakes both typographical and in content.

If you do not wish to be bound by the above, you may return book to the publisher for a full refund.

Table of Contents

When I Cook, They Run

An Introduction to the Art of Miserable Meal Making

I can cook, but I feel I was not meant to cook. I know there are people just like me, and they were not meant to cook either. Then there are others who know how to cook and, for so many reasons, from full-time work to just plain tedium, should learn not to.

For too long, society has placed so much emphasis on "good" cooking and "fine" dining as the supreme end-all of entertaining and accomplishment. Because of this, there are thousands of cookbooks on the market today that tell you every aspect of how to cook better, faster and easier.

This cookbook is different. It teaches you how not to cook, how to free yourself from the constraints of always cooking better, faster, easier. It tells how to cook using smell, look, and taste to make the meal more miserable. This cookbook introduces you to The Art of Miserable Meal Making.

The Freezer Fairy

My first awareness of my aversion to cooking came when I began to worship the Freezer Fairy. Each day when it came time to think about preparing dinner, I would find myself standing in a daze before the freezer door. I realized that I was praying that a fairy princess had secretly cooked something and left it in the freezer. I call this "freezer worship," and I was a loyal subject. But nothing edible ever emerged.

As I moved toward meal time liberation I realized that the Freezer Fairy was actually the ghost of my mother's cooking. Each day I made a pilgrimage to the freezer, just like I made the trek to her table. She always had a great meal for me, so why couldn't the Freezer Fairy do the same thing? When I finally realized that the Freezer Fairy wasn't going to deliver, I would slump to the kitchen floor to contemplate the overwhelming challenge of getting food into my own family's stomach.

When I finally landed on the hard, cold tile, reality moved me to the next issue. How long had I been waiting in vain for the Freezer Fairy, and what meal was I supposed to be preparing for my family? Had I prayed through lunch so that we were now approaching dinner? Had my trance extended through the night so that the early light of breakfast was looming on the horizon? Yet I would feel deep within me the rebellious grumbling. "I don't care what time it is," my insides would scream, "I WANT PANCAKES!" Pooh, pooh to the rules of my childhood, my tongue wants to eat ice cream before roast chicken or maybe even both at the same time. Who made these rules and why do we feel that we must eat by them?

Family Food Guilt

This first inkling of rebellion toward the established norm in the kitchen made me examine all of my long-held beliefs about cooking. When I was growing up my family preached the food lover's gospel: "Cook the best you can, prepare from scratch, make it elegant, tasty and plentiful." My relatives cooked to please. As a child all I had to do was cry, "It's too warm," "It's too cold," or "This food looks funny," and without a single word the food was whisked away and adjusted to my liking. They continue to cook to please to this very day.

Eating was—and still is—my family's main recreational sport. When we all get together, the entire visit centers around eating in large quantities. Every holiday is an around-the-clock eat fest.

Cooking–A Spectator Sport

In the beginning I, too, espoused this "food equals love" philosophy, and I tried to keep pace with my relatives in the culinary marathon. Over time, however, I discovered that this approach did not work for me.

Today I think of cooking as a sport. As in sports, not everybody has the same skill level. There are cooking professionals and there are amateurs. But most of all there are spectators, people who stand on the sidelines cheering for those who are gifted and should be participating. This is where I have found my place, and this is where I intend to stay. I consider the sport of cooking to be as dangerous as skydiving or river-rafting. To me it is much safer to be an observer than a participant.

Once I recognized that my naive desire to cook well was motivated by an overriding dose of "family food guilt," I was able to explore the liberating possibilities of freedom from the kitchen. Oh, what freedom I felt when I finally realized that cooking and taking out the garbage had the same place in my dislike column. Both were chores that I had to do, but I didn't have to like.

Writing this cookbook is my final step down the road to parole from the kitchen. And I feel so wonderfully free that I want to share my secrets with all of you who still find yourselves chained to the oven.

A quick word of advice: It is easier to camouflage the changes in your cooking with other major life changes, such as a new marriage, new job or new baby. If your family and friends cannot pinpoint a reason why you would change your cooking, they will have a hard time accepting the cooking changes. My advice is, when you are ready to make a cooking change, go out and get a job or think about having another child. It will make the transition so much easier if they think they have an explanation.

Rest assured, the information in this cookbook and the advice I give is in no way intended to harm anyone. All the recipes in this cookbook can be eaten, if they have to be. If I have done my job, your family and guests will choose not to eat them, but, just in case your relatives have no taste buds or sense of smell and are blind, the foods here are safe and edible.

Beyond the Kitchen

So now that you are about to be released, what lies beyond the kitchen? You and yours still have to eat, correct? Well there are a number of options that you may not yet have discovered. First is Home Meal Replacement. Grocery stores and restaurants have finally realized that there are a lot of people out there who would prefer someone else do the dirty work. Today, like a dream come true, they can just pick up a fully prepared meal at the grocery store. They finally have their very own Home Meal Replacement Fairy. I am so excited about this new trend that I could be the Home Meal Replacement spokesperson and poster mom.

I've written this cookbook to share my newfound freedom with others and to tell them how to join me in my liberation. Start by making a target list of those you wish to move off your table. Then make a meal-by-meal plan using the recipes in this cookbook. Execute your plan by preparing meals that are so miserable that you will never have to cook for them again! It then becomes *your* choice, if you wish to cook, not their choice that you will cook.

As you start down the road of Miserable Meal Making, remember that after reading this cookbook, you too will be able to say, "When I Cook, They Run."

Enjoy!

Karen Kallet

Profiles of Miserable Meal Makers: Are You One of Us?

I know that there are people out there who thrive on making wonderful, delicious meals. I will even admit that there are times when I want a meal to be well prepared and delicious. For instance, I make the most terrific Thanksgiving dinner every year. There are thousands of cookbooks that help me do this. However, part of the reason I do it every year is that it is expected that I will do it every year. And I know that I must protect myself from being expected to cook every night.

The first step to freedom is to recognize yourself as a potential Miserable Meal Maker. Do you hear four thousand times a day "Mommy, I'm hungry"? Have you barely had a chance to walk in the door from work before someone is saying, "What's for dinner"? Do you often think, "Why do I bother cooking? They wolf it down in five minutes, without even tasting it". Do you often think back on your wedding vows and wonder where your head was at when you promised to feed the in-laws every Sunday? If this sounds like your life, you are definitely a candidate for The Art of Miserable Meal Making.

Here are profiles of some of the people who should not cook and who would relish freedom from the culinary chores. I hope that you will find yourself among them. Once you have found yourself among the profiles that follow, you need to look at those around you who are expecting you to create wonderful, delicious meals at the drop of their jaws. Some of them will be easy to move from your table, while others will need more than a subtle hint. This cookbook offers a host of ideas for how to tell them, in no uncertain terms, that the kitchen is closed.

The Make It, Break It Bride

To be a bride or not to be a bride, the vows you take say nothing about cooking meals for the rest of your life. In fact they say for better or worse, so take the worse part to heart. Forget all that stuff your grandmother told you about the way to a man's heart being through his stomach. That might be true, but you can also get there by always being on the lookout for the newest great restaurant.

Unless you want to spend the rest of your life in the kitchen, you absolutely must make it clear from the very beginning that you are a Miserable Meal Maker. The first date is the best place to start. Invite your intended for dinner. Yes, this time you will need to cook but make sure you cook the absolutely most miserable meal you can. The first miserable meal will weed out all those potential spouses who so love good food that they don't ask you for seconds. The ones who are left, you will know love you for who you are, not for your skill in the kitchen.

Every new bride must listen carefully and hear that she has vowed to love her husband "in sickness and in health," not in food shopping, cooking and dishwashing. Caught up in the novelty of domestic bliss and charmed by the perfect man, many a bride forgets that she gives up much more than she gets when it comes to cooking. On the other hand, when she proves right away that she cannot cook, she will enjoy fewer hassles from her new husband and his family because of their low expectations.

I've never heard of a man who does not pursue a woman he is attracted to because she can not cook. On the other hand, I have heard of couples who get divorced because the husband felt neglected by the wife who didn't cook the way she used to. Learn from those mistakes; put your Miserable Meal Making cards on the table from the very beginning.

Always make the first meal the most miserable meal you can, because then you will never have to make another. A romantic first meal could include Lumpy Gray Surprise Balls (page 86), Birthday Cake Salad (page 115), Crunch and Bite Mashed Potatoes (page 104), and for dessert, Coconut Ice with Whole Kernel Corn (page 93).

One word of warning: In the flush of new love, your new partner is sure to tell you that the meal you've made is wonderful. Don't believe him. Stand tall in your conviction of its miserableness, and remember that he will say anything to make his conquest. Next thing you know he will be saying, "Let's just have a quiet dinner in tonight," and expect you to cook again. Remember that he was raised on the story his father told about how his mother couldn't cook when he first met her, and now look what a wonderful cook she turned out to be. It is a male age-old story line and you need to be strong to resist it.

Through these early examples you can prove without a doubt that cooking is not your forte. In fact, you can let him know that your exploration of this skill will be detrimental to his stomach. You will have a much easier time getting help in the kitchen, and you will hear the comforting words, "Let's eat out" with greater and greater frequency and more and more enthusiasm.

The Supper Mom: Makin', then Cookin', the Bacon...

Are you a working mom? Are you sick of arriving home to your family's whining questions about tonight's menu? If they are so hungry, why can't they whip something up themselves? Maybe it is time you made a change in the kitchen. Maybe it is time for some Miserable Meals.

Your family will be the loudest complainers about the foods they are being served. In their minds, "Mom's Kitchen" is their favorite restaurant. When your meals become miserable you will hear their howls loud and clear. And you can't blame them. Their favorite restaurant just got a new chef who doesn't make things the way they like them.

At first they will cling to the hope that things will straighten out, that this is only a phase mom is going through, that she's having a bad week. Every day they will hang around the kitchen hoping that their favorite meals and snacks will emerge from the smell and odor in mom's kitchen. After a few days they will become angry, their feelings and tastebuds bruised and wounded. In a few more days the bruises will fade and the anger will subside into dejection. "Our favorite restaurant has gone down the tubes," they will moan, unable to lift themselves out of their easy chairs to fix themselves something to eat. For a few days they will wallow in this stupor and then miraculously, they will suddenly be so hungry that they will rise up and—believe it or not—fix something for themselves! Then you will know that you've freed yourself from the culinary chains and that your time is your own.

Low Man on the Firefighter's Pole

Do not think for a moment that Miserable Meal Making is only women's salvation. Men are the real pros, for they have been perfecting these techniques for generations. We've all heard the lines: "My mother never taught me," "I have an oven, but I don't know how to turn it on," or "My wife does all the cooking, so I don't need to." In fact, most men are genetically adapted to Miserable Meal Making. They know that they have to eat and they figured out early on that they need to get someone else to prepare the food.

However, there are some men out there who are expected to cook. In fact, some have jobs that require them to cook as a part of the workplace experience. Firefighters are a good example. They are highly trained and skilled workers, but they are also asked to participate in the group firehouse meal making. It's part requirement and part tradition.

These fine men and women have not been through all that training to spend time as chief cook and bottle washer. They need to practice The Art of Miserable Meal Making from the very first meal they are asked to cook. Proving that you are a miserable cook but a great firefighter will refine the job description immediately. The best way to do this, of course, is to make sure that whatever miserable meal recipe you use creates a lot of smoke. A good recipe to try is Barbecued Pasta (page 105). Sit back and enjoy while your firefighter buddies do all the cooking.

Bachelor Ed

Bachelor Ed is my hero. Bachelor Ed has Miserable Meal Making down to a science. Year after year he has won the title King of the Miserable Meal. He is the undefeated champion and I study his technique. I'm not quite sure if he was born with this talent or if he learned it in the military or in the men's locker room in high school. Wherever it came from, it works!

Bachelor Ed comes in two types. The first always has a refrigerator devoid of anything except a few beers and frosted beer mugs. The other Bachelor Ed has an empty refrigerator, but a freezer full of food. The delicacies therein include TV dinners, frozen pizzas, and frozen candy bars.

Bachelor Ed knows all the ways to get a meal cooked for him. "Oh Jane, I'm starving for a good meal. Won't you cook me something special?" or "Oh Jane, I just want to be alone with you tonight. Why don't you come over to my place and we'll whip something up and have a nice quiet dinner." Jane falls for the romance and fails to understand that it is she that is being whipped up into being the cook.

My other favorite Bachelor Ed line is, "I don't have anything to eat, so why don't you pick something up on your way over." Only you arrive to find the kitchen so poorly equipped that you can hardly dish out the Chinese food. Even if you wanted to cook a meal you couldn't.

On the rare occasion that Bachelor Ed wants to make points and invites you to have dinner at his house and he doesn't ask you to cook, I can almost guarantee that someone else did the cooking before you got there. The "secret meal maker" might be his neighbor, friend, former girlfriend or, the most likely, his mother. When he can't find anybody to cook for him, he'll take out from the local gourmet shop, supermarket, caterer or restaurant and transfer the food into the few pots and pans he owns.

When he absolutely cannot find a cooking source, Bachelor Ed goes to Plan B. What's Plan B? A barbecue, of course! Even though Bachelor Ed may not be able to cook, he always knows how to barbecue. Somehow he does not equate barbecuing with cooking, probably because it is so much fun to play with fire. Watch closely and you will catch him squirting lighter fluid onto the already flaming coals. He will cook everything "blackened" style to cover up that he put the meat on the coals before they were ready. Don't fall for this ploy either. It is a trick he learned from his father, and his father learned from his father, and his father...

Food-Seeking Groupies

Have you ever had friends who are always looking for a free meal? Are they always showing up at your house just as you take a wonderful new dish out of the oven? It is almost as if they have been lurking in the bushes beneath the kitchen window waiting for the perfect moment to pounce on the new dish? Are they constantly hunting around in your refrigerator, looking for that last beer or getting some ice, when you know that they are really checking out the leftovers? These are the hardest friends to move from your table. They are the Food-Seeking Groupies.

The motto of the Food-Seeking Groupies is "Nobody cooks better than *you* do." They will say it to you again and again. At first you will be flattered, and you will enjoy cooking for them. You will start to invite them over when you are serving special meals or trying new recipes because their praise is so welcome and makes you feel so warm.

Then one day you will realize that you are starting to select recipes that you think they will like, that you are making their favorites again and again. Suddenly it will dawn on you that your kitchen and your life is being run by these people and they aren't even your family. They are expanding in number because they gather followers along the way. First they come as singles, then they are couples. Next thing you know the local marching band, your bowling buddies, or the kid down the street, who is always looking for a way to stay for dinner, are all standing in your kitchen waiting for you to finish cooking. The minute you even start thinking about making a meal, there they are asking, "What's for dinner?" And then it occurs to you that you have served them about 3,000 times, but not once have they returned the favor. It is definitely time to fight back.

You must take a firm stance with Food-Seeking Groupies. Make a stack of Full Pan Pancakes (page 67) and keep them in the fridge for snacks. Create Bean and Banana Sandwiches (page 75) for three days in a row. Fry up some Liver Strips (page 84) and send the aroma out the window to the bushes. You will see them streaking away in droves.

Getting rid of the Food-Seeking Groupies will help your food bill tremendously. There is no truth that two can eat as cheaply as one. Food-Seeking Groupies freeload at your expense. They eat twice as much as the occasional guest. They are no longer polite regarding portions; they think nothing of taking second or third helpings. After all, they consider themselves part of the family. The Art of Miserable Meal Making will send them packing fast.

Those Pesky Sunday Diners

Do you have family regulars that you just cannot get rid of? Are some from prior generations and you inherited them? Did they attach themselves to you at a past holiday dinner and never got up to leave?

These are some of the hardest diners to get rid of. They have a built-in mechanism to deflect any hint that they should leave your table. They hear comments such as, "Drop dead and go starve yourself," and they think that you are either talking to someone else or kidding. You couldn't possibly mean them. After all, they have been coming to your house for years.

Let me warn you: You will find that they become fussier and fussier the longer they eat with you. Some start by complimenting you on a particular dish, then asking that you make it next week. Others develop dietary restrictions, real or imagined, so that you will have to be careful what and how you prepare things. Suddenly you will find that you are developing your whole menu around what cousin Sue can and cannot eat.

For some Sunday diners, presentation becomes the key. They will only eat on heated plates, only on the dishes they gave you or only at certain times of the day. They will show up at that time whether or not you invited them for that time. The variations are vast and scary.

All the members of this group have one thing in common: They never invite you to dinner at their house.

They never offer to trade off or even share the cooking. They never bring anything except an appetite.

After a few of your Miserable Meals, however, you may suddenly hear them insisting that you come to their house. Once you are there you will find that they have made some of their old favorites, perhaps in an attempt to remind you of how they are supposed to taste. If they don't invite you over, don't worry. They are probably spending all their free time finding another segment of the family who makes more edible meals.

The logistics of the table is an important tool in deterring this group. Set your table for only the number of people you intend to serve. Put place cards at each setting, to make sure the right people get the seats and the others don't. Make sure the table is uncomfortably small and that no extra places can be squeezed in. If there is anyone feuding in your family, seat them next to each other.

Consistency is the key with this group. The family can easily understand that you have had a temporary change of heart or a touch of bad luck in the kitchen. They will expect, if not demand, that you return to your old ways as soon as they can make you. Before you know it, you are back in the same cooking situation you were in before. After all, "no one cooks better than you."

The Party Queen

Do you love to throw parties? Are you always the host for the New Year, Christmas, Thanksgiving, July Fourth, bowling league, brownie troop or Friday night get-together? Do parties always end up at your house, no matter who plans them? Do you always end up doing it all yourself, no matter how much help they told you they were going to give you? Are you always the one who works like a dog to make sure everything is perfect?

If you answered yes to two or more of these questions, you are the Party Queen. Party goers love to elevate their hostess to royalty status. They figure if they give you all sorts of praise, you will invite them again. It is politicking at its best.

Throw a Miserable Meal Making Party and watch these party goers move on faster than a flock of geese heading south for the winter. Party goers are a very fickle bunch; one bad party and they are gone for good.

Your guests will remember a bad party a lot longer than a bad meal. So this is the easiest of all the groups to get rid of. Then you can become the one raving to the hostess about what a wonderful time you are having.

Table Scrappy Pooch

Most people consider their pets to be part of the family. There is no doubt that most pets consider themselves to be part of the family. Yet, while the rest of the family gets a home-cooked meal, the family pooch gets a cold can of bow wow food, or even worse, dry nuggets. So what do they do to protest? They beg at the table. Begging was cute when they were pups, with those big sad eyes and cute yipping bark. Now the puppy has grown, and the problem has, too.

Begging is one of the most persistent undesirable behaviors that your dog will ever have. Yet who can blame them? If you knew there was something better on the table, you'd be begging, too.

I love pets, too, but I have found the sure-fire technique to stop the begging. It will only take a few miserable meals before your dog realizes that what comes from the table is much less desirable than what comes from the can. Soon your dog will look lovingly at a can of dog food. Just about any pet that persists with the bad habit of begging for table scraps can benefit from The Art of Miserable Meal Making.

One day my neighbor called asking if she could borrow some hot dogs. When I asked what for, she told me they were for her dog. She went on to explain that she was cooking hot dogs for the dog though the family was eating leftovers. This woman clearly needs to make some Miserable Meals for her dog.

The Miserable Meal Making Rules

For the meal to really excel at The Art of Miserable Meal Making, the recipe must fall into one of the three categories: Smells Bad, Looks Bad, or Tastes Bad. The more categories the recipe falls into, the higher the chance of recipe failure.

Rule #1: Smells Bad

Smell is the strongest of the five senses and it plays a huge role in how we react to things that we taste. If something that I have cooked doesn't smell the way my guests expect, it puts out a big "CAUTION" sign for them. It is the same as when you walk into a fish restaurant and the restaurant smells like low tide. You'll head quickly for the nearest exit. When food smells good, the salivary glands get worked up and the tastebuds get ready for a treat. When the food smells bad or doesn't smell as expected, the stomach starts to churn, the head turns away, and the tastebuds say, "There's no way you are putting that in this mouth."

Nothing makes guests hungrier than the aroma of wonderfully prepared food. A strong smell or a lack of aroma when one is expected is a fast way to stop guests from even trying the meal. Too much spice or too little will have the same effect. Your guests will make a judgment about the food before they even sit down at the table. When the smell is not what they are expecting or accustomed to, they will get a bit cautious about the food. For strong smellers, try Chunky Liverburgers (page 74) or Grilled Anchovy and Cheese Sandwiches (page 76).

Strong smells, such as burnt or overly spiced foods, are always good starters on the road to a miserable meal. But be careful. The strong smell of raw onions may send some people packing, but others consider it seventh heaven. Spices are effective in changing the desired outcome of a food. However, very spicy food is all the rage right now and some of my attempts at overly spiced recipes have ended up to be my family's favorites. So be sure you have some idea of the personal preferences of your guests. The Onion Chili Brick (page 88) or Deep Fried Liver Strips (page 84) will do the trick for overly spicy and smelly.

Smells can also be used to fool your guests. There are many dishes that smell wonderful, but when they bite into them they will get another story. You may want to fool your guests by having a good smell simmering when they arrive. Boil some water with cinnamon and oranges, or bake slice-and-bake cookies right before they arrive. (Then throw them out or your guests will find them and think you are a wonderful baker.) This will raise their anticipation of the meal and give them a big surprise with the first mouthful. The Chunky Beef Fruit Stew (page 89) smells really great; it's the look that is the turnoff.

Rule #2: Looks Bad

Your guests have become accustomed to, if they don't seek out, unusual-looking items that may shock their senses but please their tastebuds. There are basically three ways to make food look bad: color, texture or shape.

THE WONDERFUL WORLD OF COLOR There are many ways to change the color of a food to something unexpected. The easiest is with food coloring. Try adding a mixture of food coloring to gelatin. Or add a contrasting color to your recipe to make the dish look rather muddy. Color something that should be white, like mashed potatoes. It is fun to make them green, but it is also effective to add subtle color, such as making them just yellow enough to seem off.

You can also add bits of different colored foods to a dish that should be a particular color. For instance, add tiny pieces of green beans to your pancakes, as in the Full Pan Pancakes (page 67) or red candies to your mashed potatoes. Use color to camouflage food so your guests are presented with the unexpected. For instance, mix together potatoes, turnips and pearl onions for an all-white motif. Because all of these foods are the same color, your guests will get a big surprise with each bite.

MIX-AND-MATCH TEXTURES One of the easiest ways to create a successful Miserable Meal recipe is by altering the consistency of the food. Texture is a main component of the taste sensation. If your guests bite into a dinner roll and it is as hard as a brick, they won't take another bite of that roll. When the texture is not what they expect, they will beat a hasty retreat from the table.

Use textures to surprise your guests with each bite. Your guests have preconceived ideas as to the consistency of the foods they are about to eat. Anything that varies from the expected is less than acceptable or even down right inedible. The Brown-Crusted Moundings (page 66) or Cherry Tomato Chocolate Cake (page 94) offer a real test of texture.

Try mixing together common foods to create unusual textures. For instance, mix mashed potatoes and diced pickles. There is something about hot lumpy mashed potatoes speckled with cold cubes of pickle that will make your guests take notice. Mix watery instant mashed potatoes with cubed raw onions and water chestnuts. This is a chunky Miserable Meal treat for the eyes as well as the tastebuds.

Try mixing coconut ice shavings with frozen whole kernel corn, as in Coconut Ice with Whole Kernel Corn (page 93). Your guests' senses may be able to overcome the look and smell, but the taste and consistency will get them every time. The brain has a hard time accepting the fact that two items, such as frozen corn and ice, have been combined in a form that just doesn't look or taste right to the brain. It is like having an inner ear infection affect your balance. By mixing textures, I try to recreate that same type of imbalance in the tastebuds.

ALTERED SHAPES Cut your foods into unusual shapes, or mix together foods with contrasting shapes and textures, such as beans and fruit. Serve a hot food cool, or a cool food hot, so it has an unappetizing look and texture. Try Bean and Banana Sandwiches (page 75) or Yogurt Crouton Surprise Sandwiches (page 80) for an altered state of food.

When a food doesn't look as you expect, you immediately proceed with caution. I once ordered shrimp at a restaurant. When the shrimp came, I looked at the dish and yelled "What's this?" The waiter looked at me as though I was a complete idiot, and said, "shrimp!" I just couldn't believe my eyes, for I had never seen shrimp with heads and claws. It just ruined the meal for me.

Rule #3: Tastes Bad

Taste is the third and final tool when it comes to Miserable Meal Making. Your guests may be willing to risk an odd smell or an unusual presentation, but when the taste is not what they expect, they may try the dish, but they will not eat it.

As with smell, there is also a range in taste. The taste can be too strong or too weak taste, or no taste at all. Taste is a personal thing, and knowing the range of preference among your family and friends is key. My preference is too strong or no taste, but every person is different. For instance, I can't eat the Fried Eggs a la Shortening (page 65), but others find them "greasy" but not inedible. Onion Ice Cream with Brown Gravy Topping (page 95) is another show stopper for most people, but a few have "enjoyed" the taste surprise.

It is a toss-up which is more effective in Miserable Meal Making, taste, smell, or looks. I try to achieve at least one of the three categories in each dish I make. It is also fun to put together a menu in which each dish accomplishes a different rule. The more Miserable Meal Rules a menu follows, the more miserable the meal will turn out to be.

More Hints in the Art of Miserable Meal Making

The Miserable Meal Notebook

In the pursuit of the Miserable Meal, learn from the pros. The next time you go to a restaurant that you don't like or you are served a dish that you don't like, ask yourself to describe why you don't like the meal. Write down everything you object to in a notebook that you keep just for Miserable Meal Notes. What didn't you like about the restaurant? Was it the food, the quality, portion size, atmosphere, table service or cost? What was wrong with the dish? Did it taste bad? Smell bad? Look bad? Now try to apply those failings to the next meal that you prepare. I can guarantee that you won't have much repeat business, just as you won't be going back to that restaurant.

When I pay for a meal in a restaurant, my expectations are much higher than when I prepare my own food. When the food I am about to eat is inexpensive or free, my standards are lower and I am more willing to put up with something. Think of how many times you have said that the food at the restaurant was OK, but not worth the money. When cooking at home and trying to imitate your bad restaurant scenario, you will find your family and guests much more tolerant of your cooking, since they are not paying for the meal. So you'll need to make sure that the meal is miserable enough for them to get the message.

'Tis the Season to Season

To season or not to season, it is a big question. Seasoning has a lot to do with the success factor in any recipe. Just think of how many times have you sent food back in a restaurant because the chef used a heavy hand when seasoning your meal.

How often have you thought to yourself, "Boy, this is bland. Did the chef use any seasoning at all?" or "Boy, the chef was heavy-handed with the salt!" The first bite can ruin the whole meal when it is not seasoned properly.

My advice is always use a heavy hand with the spices. Guests can always add more spice to a dish that is too bland, but they can't change a dish that is already too spicy.

The Al Dente Factor

In regular cooking there is an acceptability factor that most good cooks are taught to strive for. It is a dish that is perfectly cooked, not over or undercooked. Italians call this "al dente." It describes the right consistency for pasta. This cookbook strives to stay as far away as possible from the "al dente factor." The good news is that this is such a narrow zone in cooking that every dish can be planned to avoid it. When you undercook it can always by accident end up al dente. So I recommend overcooking, because you can't ever go back to al dente.

Upside-down Timing

Nothing ruins a meal faster than when all the dishes are not ready at the same time or when they are served in the wrong order. Food prepared too early sits on a plate and gets cold. Cooked food takes on unusual textures when it sits around for a while. Every food has its bad side, from wilted lettuce, to separated gravy, to a crust of fat on a casserole.

Use your microwave to "finish off" a dish once it has been cooked. That extra five minutes does wonders to change the look, texture, and taste. Or cook the meal the day before, then put it in the refrigerator overnight. It will safely take on the look of food that has been sitting around.

Another technique is to change the order of the meals you serve. How many times have you heard, "No more, thanks, I'm saving room for dessert"? Why is it that we feel compelled to eat the rest of the meal first when it is really the dessert that we want? I say, break away from these antiquated "mother says" rules.

Eat in whatever order you want. Start with dessert and end with soup. When I eat in this order, I know exactly how much room I have left for the main course. Whoever said you can't eat a sandwich for breakfast, ice cream for lunch, and pancakes for dinner?

I say, eat what you want when you want it.

MIX THEM UP Changing the order of the meals you eat really makes you look differently at your cooking. For most people, dinner is the big meal of the day because it takes the most time to prepare. The world today has changed, however. As well as work, there are after-school sports, parent-teacher conferences, night school and more. Whoever gets home first and is the hungriest needs to prepare the quick meal. People are just too busy with other things to be allocating time to dinner and dining preparation.

We are so attached to the falsely imposed rules for what to eat when throughout the day that many people refuse to eat dinner for breakfast, for instance. Wouldn't it be easier to prepare a quick bowl of cereal or a frozen waffle for dinner? That doesn't sound so crazy, does it!

Stand proud and serve dessert first, announcing to your guests that you know they would save room for dessert anyway, so why not find out exactly how much. You'll see a concerned and puzzled look cross their faces, but they dare not question your reasoning.

Another technique is to serve your meal in whatever order the food is ready, but only one dish at a time. Dinner might consist of dessert, then vegetable, then bread, then appetizer, then the main dish and the soup and so on. Enhance the discombobulating nature of this technique by serving the meal late. I achieve this by not starting to cook until the guests arrive, and then cooking each dish only after the previous one has been served and eaten—or at least tasted.

Just think how miserable a meal could be if you offered the mashed potatoes and the peach cobbler at the same time, followed by the roast and the soup, and finally the vegetables. I can guarantee that your guests will be so confused by the end of the evening that they will never want to return. If the recipes don't get them, the serving style certainly will.

THE MYSTERY MEAL Then there is the mystery meal, the meal that never comes. Your guests wait so long for the meal that they leave without eating. This can be achieved with food that takes a long time to cook, such as turkey. Start the cooking so the meal will be done somewhere between midnight and 3:00 a.m. Apologize for getting such a late start, and don't be surprised when they offer to take you out to dinner.

Natural Sources for Miserable Meal Makings

Miserable Meal Making employs as many processed, store-bought, prepared foods as possible. Anything frozen, canned or prepackaged makes an easy and great Miserable Meal. Many frozen and canned foods are already pretty bad tasting, bad looking and bad smelling to begin with. That means there is not much you need to do except serve them. I stick with the old classics I remember as a kid, such as canned, dried, potted or pickled meat products. Straight out of the can or jar, they are naturally the makings of Miserable Meals.

The next time you go to the grocery store, keep an eye out for the Miserable Meal Makings that so many manufacturers have already provided you. Make notes in your Miserable Meal Notebook. A Miserable Meal is just a heat-and-serve away.

Goin' Wild with Portion Control

Portion control is an important tool for me, and my advice is go big. When guests or family members receive only a small portion they may try to hide the fact that they do not like the food. They spread it around on their plates and then claim they had plenty and are very full.

Don't give them this camouflage. Always make plenty of food and fill their plates. This way there is no way they can fool you into believing that they have had enough.

My Miserable Meal Making mission is to make a point. The point is, I am tired of cooking, I don't want to do this anymore, and since you haven't gotten my more subtle hints, this is the final straw. To drive this point home, I start a meal by stating to my guests that I feel that everyone at my table should eat everything on their plates. If their plates are heaping, this works the very first time and seldom needs to be said again.

I will admit that under certain circumstances you might want to use the opposite strategy—serve a very tiny portion to each person. I had a friend who was a master of Miserable Meal Making and didn't even know it. She used this method very effectively. At one meal, she served one chicken breast between four people. I never knew if the food was good, since I never got enough to form an opinion. After that I knew that I needed to eat before coming to their house.

Repetitive Dining

Variety in meals has always been a sore spot for me. When I had only been married a year, my boss's wife asked me during a dinner party if I could cook. I proudly assured her that I could. (I was still quite naive and under the false impression that any bride worth her weight in salt should be able to cook.) To lend credibility to my claim I mentioned that I had three specialty dishes. When she asked what they were, to my horror I could only remember two, and they both involved hamburger meat and a jar of spaghetti sauce. After that, the poor woman never expected an invitation to dinner.

When you can't bear to cook another Miserable Meal but your guests and family still haven't taken the hint and run for the hills, try repetitive dining. The basic premise of this technique is to cook a good meal that will feed your family and guests for a week, and then just keep serving it over and over. Your family and friends will not mind leftovers the first or maybe even the second night, but by the third and fourth nights they will be complaining. Anything after that is like a bad broken record. The same meal gets on their nerves until they must do something to change it.

You need to do some planning to make this technique work. Calculate how much you will need to buy to make sure that the meal lasts all week. Allow plenty of time to prepare the meal the first time, since you are making such large quantities. Remind yourself that once you have prepared the first of the meals, all the other meals will take less than ten minutes to heat and serve.

Repetitive Dining Menus from Around the World

Here's a typical week's worth of repetitive dining for a typical family of four.

THE AMERICANA FEAST Basic elements: 20 lb. turkey, stuffing, potatoes, vegetables, gravy, rolls

Day 1 Full meal with all elements served.

Day 2 Leftover meal, all elements served.

Day 3 Turkey sandwiches served open face with gravy. Use leftover rolls and turkey.

Day 4 Turkey soup with vegetables. Use the turkey bones and the leftover vegetables to make the turkey soup.

Day 5 Stuffing pockets with turkey in the middle. Bake in the oven until a crust forms on the stuffing.

Day 6 Turkey salad.

Day 7 Turkey cubes in gravy with potato dumplings.

THE ITALIAN FESTIVAL Basic elements: Meatballs, sausage, pasta sauce, pasta, salad, broccoli, and garlic bread.

Day 1 Full meal with all elements served.

Day 2 Pasta with primavera sauce. The primavera is broccoli on top of pasta with pasta sauce poured over.

Day 3 Meatball and sausage open-face sandwiches. Use the garlic bread as the base.

Day 4 Sausage salad.

Day 5 Full meal with all the elements.

Day 6 Meat sauce with pasta. Make the meat sauce with the meatballs.

Day 7 Italian soup. Use any leftovers in a soup.

THE MIDDLE EASTERN CELEBRATION Basic elements: Leg of lamb, pita bread, saffron rice, tomatoes, onions and green peppers.

Day 1 Full meal with all elements served.

Day 2 Leftover elements served.

Day 3 Lamb patties with rice.

Day 4 Lamb kabobs. Made with onions, tomatoes and green peppers.

Day 5 Pita bread stuffed with lamb and rice.

Day 6 Shaved lamb with green peppers and onions.

Day 7 Lamb soup. Use any leftovers in the soup.

If your family and friends still don't get the message after a week's worth of these ideas, repeat the week's worth of menus for a month. That should really drive home the message, "I don't want to cook anymore." And the message to you will be "Please, please don't cook for us any more."

The Final Straw: Table Setting and Service

The way you set your table can truly make the difference between a miserable meal and an okay meal. Start by always serving the meal from the bowls, pots and pans that you prepared it in. There is something about cooked food residue that doesn't bother the cook, but really bothers the guests.

No matter how beautiful they are, put away all of your china plates and cups and use only paper and plastic. Try washing and reusing your paper and plastic plates. The more they are used and then washed, the more unusual they become. If you can't bring yourself to serve on used paper plates, try covering them with plastic wrap for the second go round. Or try plastic or foam plates. They are sturdier and will wash up nicely, but they do show knife and fork marks.

Another last straw idea is to make your guests eat on their laps, especially with hard-to-cut foods on paper or plastic plates. Have you ever tried to cut a steak with a plastic knife? Sawing is in order, especially if it is made with the miserable techniques in Flank Steak a la Shoe Leather (see page 83). Make sure that you eat where the dining room table is in plain sight, but it is piled so high with old mail and newspapers that they couldn't eat at it.

Make it clear from the moment they enter your home that you expect your guests to clean up after the meal. It's always interesting to see their reaction when they find out they are expected to wash paper and plastic plates. You will need to watch them carefully, since they will try to throw out at least one of the plates while you are not looking. They most likely will walk out at this point.

When I do use my "real" dishes, I make sure the beverage glasses have water spots on them. I live in an area with very hard water and where water spots are a way of life. The best technique I've found for creating water spots is to hand wash them but don't rinse them well and use tepid water. There will be a lot of water and soap in the glasses that will leave marks when they dry. To cause great spots, leave a slight bit of water on the inside of the glass, then lay it on its side so the water dries and leaves a nice big white water stain. My husband calls this cruddy residue "cup fungus." In our house he makes it standard procedure to wash a glass before you put any liquid into it.

Be creative with what you choose to serve liquids in. Jelly jars are an old favorite of mine, but you can have a lot of fun with a more unusually shaped jar. Your guests will be challenged by dealing with the ridged lip of the jar, and they will come up with innovative ways to hold them.

You might also consider making your own drinking glasses. The most unusual homemade drinking glasses I've seen are glass soda bottles with the bottom section sawed off and the cut edge polished. The glass is very thick and heavy, but it is a definite conversation piece.

When I do use regular plates, silverware and glasses, I mismatch. Make sure every guest gets a different kind of plate. I also mix different sizes and patterns and materials, such as china, metal and plastic. The more cracks and chips a plate has, the more I cherish it. I mix it with an assorted collection of glasses and plastic forks and knives to create a very effective Miserable Meal Table Setting.

Those Darn Place Mats

I like to use table linen substitutes, such as burlap or plastic shower curtains, to add an extra sensory experience to my guests' meals. With each menu, I decide what effect I am going after. Am I looking for shock value or a real gross-out look? Remember, though, you are looking to enhance a Miserable Meal, not set the next trend in table setting design. When your guests see your table, they should feel like running as fast as they can in the opposite direction. I've had good luck with setting the table right on top of the old mail and newspapers as the place mats and tablecloth. Then when the meal is over, I push everything into the trash.

A Centerpiece of Mind

Create a centerpiece for your table that has the look and feel of your meal. For instance, I have made my centerpieces from the cans from which the meal came. I've also used plastic wrap and foam plates from the butcher (new, of course) for an interesting display. With a little creativity and an open mind, the combinations are limitless.

No matter what the material, the centerpiece is sure to be a conversation starter. My guests sometimes can't quite figure out what the centerpiece is made of. I have heard them say, "This centerpiece reminds me of something. Now what was it? Oh yes? Oh no! It can't be. It is!"

Stove-Top Buffet

My personal favorite method of serving meals is the stove-top buffet. Just invite your guest into the kitchen and give them a plate and let them serve themselves directly from the stove. Leave all the food in the cooking pots and pans and have the guests scoop their food from the pots.

To prepare the kitchen for a stove-top buffet you must not wash any of the dishes you used for cooking. The counter tops should be covered with assorted objects such as food boxes, chip bags, empty soda cans, dish rags and sponges. Scatter the counter with things that don't necessarily relate to the food: old bills, catalogs, newspapers, receipts, or the laundry.

THE ONE-POT MEAL You can also try the one pot meal, where all the food is cooked and served in one pot. This includes the appetizer, main dish and even the dessert.

There are two ways to approach the one-pot meal. The first way is to cook all the items in the pot at the same time. It creates a very strange-looking stew.

The other way is to use the one pot to cook each of the dishes and then leave the residue from the last dish in the pot to flavor the next dish. Depending on what you cook, you can end up with some very innovative flavor combinations.

Serving with No Style

Your serving technique is also very important in making a miserable meal memorable. Slop the food on the plate, like at a charity hall dinner or in the military. Be sure to pour the gravy over everything, including your guest. Serve yourself first, then tell your guests that they can help themselves to what's left. Serve the food in a way that catches your family and guests off guard and make them wish that they had eaten somewhere else.

Mood Meals

The mood at your meal is very important. Set the mood by having the television blaring and the neighborhood kids playing loudly in the next room. Invite the family dog to beg for scraps (unless the dog has already discovered that human meals are miserable). Or better yet, invite the dog onto your lap or even onto the table during the meal. Pay no attention when he eats from the serving pots, but nonchalantly pass the leftovers to your guests. Have a camera nearby to record the horrified looks on their faces.

The more disruptive you make the mood around the dinner table, the more horrified your guests will be. Be sure that you play loud, fast music while you are eating. Ask a fellow Miserable Meal Maker to call you right in the middle of dinner. Bring the portable phone to the table and talk loudly for as long as possible. A few minutes after you've hung up, remember something you forgot to tell her and call her back. Pass the serving pots continually throughout the meal so that the guests must constantly pass them on. Change the subject often, interrupting any conversations that are ongoing.

Location, Location, Location

The location of where family or guests regularly eat is very important and comfortable to them. You may want to move to a new and unusual eating place. Move your table into the laundry room, the bedroom, or put it out in the front yard. Put the kids at the adult table and make the adults eat at the kids' table or at rickety card tables.

Position the table in a high traffic area so your guests are constantly required to get up to let someone by. Seat your guests at the kitchen counter where there is no leg room. Then cram the counter top with so many things that there is no room for their plates.

The most unusual place to serve a meal is in the bathroom. I seriously doubt that your family and guests will handle it. If they don't seem too bothered by the idea of eating in the bathroom, choose a special moment to ask them all to leave so that you can ... well, I bet you can imagine.

Many people love to eat outdoors, so be sure that you prepare the area properly if this is where you choose to stage your meal. Water the ground under the eating area just before your guests arrive. This will assure that bugs and birds and whatever else lives in your yard will be awake and doing their annoying best to entertain your guests or family. The smell of the food cooking and a few crumbs on the ground will be sure to attract critters such as ants and flies and even skunks and squirrels, who love to eat right off the table.

Barbecue smoke drives away a lot of bugs and animals, but if it is thick enough it can smoke out your guests and family as well. In the summer the evening hours can bring mosquitoes. Serve them a delicacy—your guests. If you live in an area of the country that doesn't have mosquitoes, I'm sure you can think of an equally annoying pest. These little predators, such as flies and gnats, can do more to get rid of your guests than anything you can think of.

In cold or rainy climates, when no one wants to be outside, have a winter picnic. It will be one of the fastest meals you have ever served. Your family and guests will eat and be out of there in a flash. In hot climates serve meals in the heat of the day with no air-conditioning or fans. The heat gets them moving every time, usually without taking a bite.

You must be careful not to overdo it with mood and atmosphere. Your family and guests may find the changes delightful or hysterically funny. They may want to stay longer or come back sooner, because it was one of the best times they have ever had. Carefully analyze the guests you are cooking for and set the appropriate mood to create the best Miserable Meal atmosphere for that group.

The "I Cooked, You Clean" Mantra

The clean-up is your final line of Miserable Meal offense. When you have done all the things suggested in the previous pages and haven't gotten the desired results, you will with the clean-up process. Tell your guests and family that there is one basic rule in your kitchen: "If I cook, you clean up."

Stop yourself from doing any clean up while you are cooking and even the most normal amount of pots and pans will look like a mound by the time the meal is over. This should discourage even the most stubborn of eaters. It will make them more considerate when it comes to asking you what you are going to make them to eat. Consistently follow this rule, since they will encourage you not to cook just so they do not have to clean up. They will begin to carefully weigh what they get against what they have to do, and find that it is not worth it.

It is an art to create a mountain of dishes. To properly create this mountain, never use the same pot or pan twice when doing your cooking. Always pile the dishes into the sink without the sink stopper being inserted. This is so that the person cleaning up has to dig through the dirty dishes to get to the drain. It gives them an impending feeling of doom, if they already didn't feel it from the meal itself. Another technique is to slip the dirty dishes into a sink full of cold, soapy water. The water will become greasy and slimy and the dishwasher will have to pull the plug to fill the sink with new water. Plunging one's hand into cold, greasy water has got to be one of life's most unpleasant tasks.

If you have an automatic dishwasher, tell your guest washer that the dishwasher doesn't work. If it is full of clean dishes, tell them that you use it for storage. When you've used paper and plastic plates, tell your guests to hand wash them since the dishwasher has a tendency to eat them up.

When you don't feel you have created enough dishes for your guest washer to wash, invent some. There must be a pot, pan, plate or dishes that you have been meaning to clean. This will arouse suspicious looks from your guest washers, especially when they can't remember using the dishes they are washing.

When you are serving guests instead of family, it will be the final blow when you ask them to clean up. Don't be surprised if many of them become suddenly ill and hustle their way out of your house. They are not likely to return—at least not to eat and clean up!

This strategy can backfire on you, if it is used on an ongoing basis. I now have to promise my husband that I will clean up certain meals that are my personal favorites. He doesn't think any of my meals are worth preparing, especially if he has to clean up. He would much rather eat out then have to clean up from a meal he dislikes.

Miserable Meal Making Hints for Cooking and Baking

It is easy to fail at cooking and baking—if you know how. Follow these suggestions and your attempts will be miserable every time.

Cooking Failures

If you adopt the Miserable Meal philosophy when you cook, then even the simplest food can be changed to a Miserable Meal, with no hassle or special ingredients.

MISERABLE MEATS

- For miserably fried meats, make sure the fat is not hot.
- For meat that is browned unevenly, overcrowd the pan.
- For meat with a smoky, burnt flavor, barbecue it when the flame is roaring.
- For tough meat, brown the meat in a pan that has not been preheated.

MISERABLE VEGETABLES

- For soggy vegetables, let them sit in the water in which they were cooked.
- For mushy vegetables, overcook them. Twenty minutes for every two is recommended.
- For hard vegetables, cook ½ minute for every 2 recommended.

MISERABLE EXTRAS

- For mushy spaghetti, let the spaghetti sit in the water in which it was cooked.
- For dried out and clumpy spaghetti, let the drained but not rinsed spaghetti sit for about 20 minutes before serving.
- For greasy gravies and stews, do not skim the layer of grease that forms on top.
- For a roast that has cooking residue hanging from it, leave the pan drippings with the roast.
- For poorly seasoned food, cook the food with no seasoning, then add herbs and spices after the dish is cooled.

Miserable Baking Messes

Some of the easiest failures come from baking. Follow these failure tips and even the best recipe will become a miserable one. It can be as easy as over-beating or adding too much of a certain ingredient. Most cookbooks would include these in things to avoid or how to learn from your mistakes. I include them as things you should study and apply to as many recipes as possible.

MISERABLE PIES

- For crumbled pastry, over-mix the flour and the fat.
- For tough pastry, use too much water and over-mix the dough.
- For pie that is not brown, do not bake in glass or enamel pans. Bake the pie at an uneven temperature.

MISERABLE BREADS

- For bread that is too holey, bake the bread at a too low temperature. Or let the bread over-rise.
- For bread with a crust that is dark and has blisters, under-rise the dough. The crust and the bread will blister just under the crust.
- For bread that won't rise, use old yeast or over-knead the bread.
- For bread that is streaky, knead the bread unevenly or under-knead the bread.
- For uneven bread, use old dark pans or put too much dough in the pan. Cook at a too high temperature or crowd the bread too tight on the oven shelf.

MISERABLE CAKES

- For cracked and uneven cake, add too much flour or bake in a too hot or too cool oven.
- For dry cake, use too much flour, too little shortening, too much baking powder or cook the cake at a too low temperature.
- For a heavy cake, more commonly known as the lead sinker, use too much sugar and bake for a shorter period of time than specified.
- For cake with a sticky crust, use too much sugar.
- For coarse cake, mix very little, use too much fat, use too much baking soda, use fat that is too soft and bake at a low temperature.

CAKE FREE FALL

- For cake that falls, under-bake, use too much sugar, too much fat, too little baking soda and not enough flour.
- For cake that is browned unevenly, bake at too high a temperature, crowd the pan and use old uneven pans.
- For a cake with uneven color, do not mix well.

MISERABLE MUFFINS

- For coarse muffins, cook at a too high temperature and over-mix the batter.
- For muffins with tunnels, over-mix and add too much water to the recipe.
- For generally miserable muffins, over-mix, bake at a too high or too low temperature.

MISERABLE BISCUITS

- For biscuits that are unevenly brown, use a dark surface pan, cook at a too high temperature and roll the dough thinly.
- For too dry biscuits, handle the biscuits a lot while you are rolling them, then cook them at too low a temperature for too long a time.
- For coarse biscuits, do not mix enough.

The Miserable Meal Making Glossary

If you closely examine the terms commonly used by cooks, you will discover that they reveal the violent nature of the sport of cooking. The words themselves are harsh and uncaring. To me that says there is something not so nice going on. Let's take a look at the following list of terms and their miserable meanings and you will see what I am talking about.

Baste Spoon fatty grease over the recipe.

Blanch What your face will look like when you cut your finger with a knife.

Degrease Hosing down the kitchen after a miserable meal.

Dredge Drag up your old feelings about cooking.

Flame Setting your food on fire.

Fold When you give up cooking and can't take it any longer.

Jumped What your guests feel like after a miserable meal.

Macerate What your stomach does when you have too much liquor and fruit at dinner.

Marinate Mix ingredients to change the taste of what you want to cook.

Mince Telling your guests very specifically to leave your table.

Reduce When you limit the amount of people who eat at your table.

Scald The no-mans-land between cooking and Miserable Meal Making. Just before something begins to boil, it is scalding.

Sear How you feel when someone tells you they liked what you served.

Shred What you will do with your collection of cookbooks and recipes after you read this book.

Strain What cooking does to you after a while.

Miserable Kitchen Designs

The roots of kitchen design originate in the days when the woman's place was in the home and primarily in the kitchen. In earlier times the kitchen was the central gathering place for the family. It was where they got warm, ate, bathed and gathered for entertainment.

When families needed more space, the parlor was created. When they outgrew that room, the dining room was created. When they outgrew the dining room the family room/den was created. The basement was finished to accommodate the expanding needs of today's families. In the past the bathroom used to be an outhouse. Then plumbing was brought indoors, but most homes only had one bathroom. Now it is standard for homes to have two or three bathrooms. Houses used to have barns. These were turned into carports and garages, which led to one-, then two-, then three-car garages. People nowadays never stop to think how excessive it is to have a home with three bathrooms and a three-car garage.

However, despite all these changes and enlargements, the kitchen layout and the kitchen's role in the house has basically stayed the same since the Middle Ages. Yes, there has been some modernization and electric appliances have been added, but generally speaking the idea of the kitchen has not been revised to meet the changes in today's society.

Miserable Meal Making will make this even more obvious to you. Your kitchen invites people over and asks them to sit and watch you cook. It is warm and cozy and encourages conversation while you work. It still has the table where friends and family gather to work and play. It is still the warmest, most welcoming room in the house.

It is time that the kitchen was redesigned to be more functional for today's Miserable Meal Makers. I propose that the entire layout of a home be changed so that the kitchen is always positioned in the front of the house. The kitchen would have an oven with a double door, one door on the inside of the house and another on the outside the house. This would allow cooking company to come by, unlock your outside oven door, put the food in the oven and turn it on. You would have a wonderful, fully cooked meal when you got home. It would be the next generation of Home Meal Replacements; you don't go out to get them, they come to you.

In older homes, the kitchens were large, but as time went on the kitchens have become smaller and smaller. We are now at the point where kitchens in some homes and apartments are the size of hall closets. This is probably the best size, especially when you don't want to cook. My preference in kitchen design would be more of an entertainment and serving hub and less of a kitchen.

Have you ever noticed that at most parties everybody ends up in the kitchen? Even if the food is in the other room, people still like to congregate in the kitchen. My theory is that the best lighting is in the kitchen. People have a tendency to gravitate away from mood lighting and into the brighter lights of the kitchen. The next time you have people over, turn off the kitchen lights and turn on a bright light in another room and watch where the crowd gravitates.

The Clean Stuff

FLOORS I hate to tell you, but I think you already know that there is no such thing as a no-wax floor. The phrase "no wax" is an overstatement. "No wax" means that you only need to wash the floor with soap and water to get it bright and shiny again. Not exactly. After a few cleanings the floor becomes dull. That's when you find out that you have to dress your no-wax floor with a special liquid that puts the shine back on the floor. This finish lasts for a couple of weeks. Who are they kidding? If you have to dress the floor with this special liquid, what's the difference?

When I realized that no-wax flooring is out as a good material for easy kitchen care, I tried tile. Tile is supposed to last forever, looks good and add to the value of the home. But there are a few things that should be considered before you put in a tile floor. The first is never attempt to install the tile yourself. It's just not worth the time, pain, blood, sweat and tears of installation. Tiling is like cooking; consider it a dangerous sport and never attempt to do it yourself or with someone you care for.

The word is that a tile floor is easy to clean and requires no special dressings. Just use water and vinegar. Most kitchen floors get pretty dirty between moppings. No matter what kind of mop you use, the dirt gets spread as a milky film on the tile. Even worse are the water spots that form on the tile floor. To get rid of the spots you must get down on your hands and knees to hand rub the water spots dry.

The tile grout is the other part of the tile story. It has a tendency to stain even if you have it sealed. There is also a problem with grout cracking and chipping. The final blow is when the tile cracks from things falling from the counter to the floor, then you are in big trouble. Let me warn you now. When you go to find replacement tiles, they are always discontinued. This means you either have to live with cracked tiles, replace the entire floor or mismatch the tiles.

Floors naturally make the kitchen a Miserable Meal Making event. No matter what you do, it will never be the way you want it.

LOVING A DIRT FLOOR, NOT A DIRTY FLOOR Because of the shortcomings of no-wax and tile floors, my hope is that there will be a new trend in kitchen flooring. Dirt floors, resurrected from the colonial days, should come back into fashion. Dirt is not half the work of any other floor you could put in and you never have to worry about hurting it. If you dig a hole in it or drop something on it, just sweep some more dirt over it. You never have to make excuses with a dirt floor. A herd of elephants could march through and you and your guests would never know it.

WALLS The walls of the kitchen are also very interesting. No matter how you try to keep a kitchen clean there are always food particles stuck to the wall somewhere. You can get the strongest cleanser you can find, one packed with ammonia or bleach, and there will still be greasy streaks and chunky splats on your walls. Sometimes you can't even pick the splats off with your fingernail.

My idea of the perfect kitchen wall is one that you can hose down with a high-volume water spray. You have seen this at the local butcher shop. The walls should be made from a material similar to that of prefab shower stalls, with no seams where the dirt can hide.

COUNTERTOPS Counter tops are supposed to be easy to clean. My experience is that all they do easily is scratch. You have to use special soaps and cloths to keep them from scratching, but you can never find the cloth when you have a spill. So you use the regular cloth or sponge and before you know it the counter top has become so scratched, it doesn't make a difference if it is clean or dirty.

SINK The other sore spot in the kitchen is the ring around the sink. This is the repository for all kinds of living, growing gunk. Even if you are the most meticulous kitchen cleaner, food particles are pushed into the ring of the sink, where they multiply and fester. It becomes a deep-down grime that has to be removed by taking a toothpick and running it around the edge of the sink to get the dirt and grease out of those hard to get to places. It is the worst job in the kitchen and is the best chore you can give to someone you want to move on from your kitchen.

My Perfectly Miserable Kitchen

My vision of the kitchen of the future is one designed for minimum maintenance. It has a pass-through oven with a door on the outside so that kind food fairies could leave fully cooked meals. The kitchen floor is covered with dirt. The walls are pre-formed acrylic, and the room is dimly lighted to discourage congregating by family and friends. Now doesn't that seem like a place you would like to stay away from? That is exactly the point.

Non Appetit!!

I hope these tips for The Art of Miserable Meal Making will help you make unsuccessful meals every time. But don't forget to be creative. For every idea I've mentioned, there are probably one thousand more. Try a few of these ideas and run with them. Soon you will find that you have rid yourself of all those pesky friends, relatives and guests that never appreciated your efforts all these years.

The Recipe to the Art of Miserable Meal Making

Each of these recipes has been developed in my kitchen or was contributed by someone else who has my sense of what qualifies as a Miserable Meal. Each recipe has been taste tested by a panel of family and friends, all of whom would prefer that I never cook for them again. I asked them to give me honest opinions about these recipes, and they were not shy in giving me an earful. Now they are very open about preferring to eat out when we get together. I wonder where they ever got that idea?

If any of these recipes is a take-off on your prized family favorite, my apologies. So far I have not found anyone who wants to own up to developing a dish that has been rated awful enough to be a Miserable Meal Making recipe. I hope that this book will give you the courage to stand proud as a Miserable Meal Maker.

I encourage you to experiment and develop your own Miserable Meal Making recipes. A good place to start is at the back of your recipe box, where you stuff any recipes you've tried and rejected with a big "X" through them.

If you do come up with something new and innovative, drop me a line. Miserable Meal Making recipes have been hard to find, and I'm always on the lookout for new ideas. I will be happy to credit you in the next edition of *When I Cook, They Run.* Step out of the cupboard and experience for yourself the freedom that Miserable Meal Making brings.

The Critics Choice Ratings:

My panel of taste testers rated each of the recipes on a scale of 1 to 5.

The judges, who have been through enough already and will remain nameless, used the following rating scale:

Rating #1: It's not so bad. I can eat a little bit of this—if you insist.

Rating #2: Well, that's different.

Rating #3: Oh my, what is that!

Rating #4: You want me to eat that? Yuck!

Rating #5: That's disgusting! I wouldn't eat that for all the money in the world.

Of course, the greatest compliment is when, at the end of the meal, one of your guests says, "That is the most Miserable Meal I have ever eaten."

Have fun, enjoy—especially when your family and friends have moved on to someone else's table!

Breakfast

Fried Eggs a la Shortening

Critics choice rating – 3

This dish is ideal for breakfast, lunch or dinner. It will leave your guests with a fast food taste in their mouths. This recipe is particularly effective on women and older relatives.

3 tbsp. shortening
4 eggs
Dash of salt

Heat frying pan on medium high and melt shortening. Swish the pan to evenly coat the bottom with shortening. Break the eggs and plop them into the pan. Fry them until they are golden brown (like French fries) on the bottom. Turn the eggs and cook until they are golden brown on the other side. Remove pan from heat and let cool for 5 minutes. Sprinkle with salt after the eggs have cooled, and serve.

HINTS: *Egg yolks break easily when plopped into the pan, making the eggs very rubbery. Adding the salt after the eggs have cooled means the salt remains crystallized on the surface of the eggs and is crunchy.*

SERVING SUGGESTIONS: You can also chill the eggs for an hour before serving, then top them with nondairy dessert topping. Breakfast and afternoon tea in one—Yum!

Makes 4 servings

Brown-Crusted Moundings

Critics choice rating – 5

A one-pan breakfast perfect for those who can't decide between eggs and cereal. This dish is so unbelievable that all new brides should make it the morning after their wedding night. The taste is indescribable. Some new husbands might be brave enough to ask what it is; most won't dare.

- 2 tbsp. oil
- 4 eggs
- 1 cup milk
- 1 cup toasted rice cereal
- 3 tbsp. grape jelly
- 1 tsp. salt and pepper to taste

Place oil in fry pan over medium heat. Break the eggs into a bowl and mix them with the milk. Pour the egg/milk mixture into the pan and scramble it until the eggs are cooked to your liking. Take the pan off the stove and mix in the cereal and grape jelly. Blend until the mixture is a brownish color. Add salt and pepper. Serve in mounds on the plate.

HINTS: *Add more grape jelly if the color is not brown enough for your taste. Add more cereal for a chunkier texture.*

Makes 4 servings

Full Pan Pancakes

Critics choice rating – 2

This recipe uses double the amount of pancake mix indicated on the box, which makes pancakes as heavy as bricks. To change the taste and texture, try imaginative additives, such as drained canned green beans, baked beans, water chestnuts, grapes, grapefruit slices, lemon peel or dill seed.

3 cups of pancake mix
1 egg
1 tsp. oil
1 cup water
2 tbsp. shortening

Mix together the pancake mix, egg, oil and water. Heat the shortening in a frying pan over high heat until it is spattering hot. Pour enough pancake mixture into the frying pan to cover the entire bottom. Mix with a whisk. Continue to whisk until chunks appear. Fry until brown on the bottom, approximately 3 minutes, then turn the pancake over and cook the other side, approximately six minutes. Remove from heat and set aside to cool.

HINTS: *The bottom of this pancake has a tendency to get burnt. If this happens, add more shortening and increase the heat for that crispy, greasy look.*

SERVING SUGGESTIONS: Make one pancake per person, and cook them all before you call anyone to the table. That way they will be nice and cold by the time your guests try to butter them.

Makes 6 servings

Bacon in Cold Chocolate Sauce

Critics choice rating – 5

This dish has the most impact at breakfast, but it can be easily used as a course in any meal. The salty bacon with the sweet topping is an "interesting" combination, to say the least. However, don't hesitate to try variations on the topping. Suggestions are: barbecue sauce, whipped cream, marshmallow topping, cream cheese or apple sauce.

1 lb. bacon
6 oz. chocolate sauce

Cook bacon in a frying pan until slightly soggy. Drain and set aside to cool. Chill the chocolate sauce in the refrigerator until firm. Place the cooled bacon on a plate and scoop the chocolate topping on the bacon. Serve at once.

HINTS: *This recipe can also be created with a variation of hot bacon. The bacon is cooked very crispy and served with heated chocolate sauce—a "bacon sundae."*

Makes 8 servings

Omelet a la Dog Track

Critics choice rating – 4

This dish has a doggie do-do look to it, which your guests will not believe. The tubular shape, the lumpiness and the color all add up to a home run from the dog track.

4 eggs
3 tbsp. mustard
1 cup bean sprouts
1 cup raisins
3 tbsp. barbecue sauce
2 tsp. water
1 tbsp. oil
1 lb. ground beef

In a bowl mix together the eggs, mustard, bean sprouts, raisins, barbecue sauce and water. Set aside. Brown the ground beef, leaving it in clumpy lumps. Let cool. When the meat is cool, add it to the omelet mixture. In a frying pan over medium, heat the oil, then pour in enough of the omelet mixture to make an omelet approximately 6 inches in diameter. Roll the pan from side to side to create a cigar shaped omelet. Serve immediately.

HINTS: *Serve this recipe hot and steaming. Use your imagination and experiment with other shapes.*

Makes 8 servings

Ten Ton Muffin

Critics choice rating – 2

This muffin looks like the grand daddy of all muffins. It is large, hard and heavy.

1 pkg. muffin mix
4 eggs
Oil as indicated on the package
Half the water indicated on the package
Any other ingredient as indicated on the package

Preheat oven to time indicated on the package. In a bowl mix together the muffin mix, eggs, oil and water. Mix well. Bake as a loaf in a high-sided cake pan, following the time and temperature indicated on the package. If not firm, bake for another 10 minutes and test again until firm.

HINTS: *If you are concerned that the muffins will not be heavy enough, add 2 cups of cereal or oatmeal to the recipe.*

Makes 8 servings

Lunch

Sweet-and-Sour Turkey Sandwiches

Critics choice rating – 5

A simplification of the after-Thanksgiving favorite—hot turkey sandwiches swimming in gravy. Your guests will be begging you to take them off the table.

½ lb. thinly sliced turkey breast
8 slices white bread
1 jar of Chinese sweet-and-sour sauce

Preheat oven to 300 degrees. Place the sliced turkey breast in a baking dish, separating the slices, and warm it in the oven for 20 minutes. While turkey is heating, warm the sweet-and-sour sauce in a pan on the stove. Place several slices of dried turkey on each piece of bread. Pour sauce over each sandwich and serve.

HINTS: *Have the turkey sliced as thin as possible, almost shaved. Choose a white bread that has a foam rubber look and texture, and a very bright red, thick sweet-and-sour sauce. For variety, substitute cornbread or another sweet bread or sliced donut. That will make it an even more Miserable Meal.*

Makes 4 servings

Chunky Liverburgers

Critics choice rating – 4

The chunky texture of this burger and the red color will stop your guests short, no matter how hungry they are. When they ask, "What is this?," list the ingredients with excitement. They are sure to nod their heads and wag their tongues when you reveal that they contain liver, for they will now recognize that obnoxious smell coming from your kitchen. Rejoice if they push the plate away without even trying a bite.

½ lb. liver
½ lb. ground beef
1 can red sliced beets
2 slices white bread

Fry the liver in a pan until firm. Let cool and cut into 1-inch chunks. Mix together the ground beef, liver squares and beets with juice. Stir until mixture is uniformly red. Break the bread into pieces and gently fold into the liver mixture. Form mixture into patties. Fry in a frying pan or grill over medium hot coals.

HINTS: *These burgers should be deep red, so do not add anything that will diminish the impact of the beet juice. The spongy liver squares mixed with the burger create a texture that will make your guests cringe. The intense red color could lead to interesting theme variations. Add canned French-style green beans for a holiday burger. Make them heart-shaped for Valentine's day. Substitute potato sticks for the bread to give a crunch among the sponginess.*

Makes 4 servings

Mashed Bean and Banana Sandwiches

Critics choice rating – 4

This is actually a pretty good sandwich. The combination of foods and the way it looks is what makes it a Miserable Meal recipe. It is messy, lumpy and greasy.

16 slices white bread
2 tbsp. margarine
4 ripe bananas
1 can baked beans

Toast the bread until slightly burnt on the edges. Spread margarine on the toast. Mash the bananas and spread on 8 pieces of bread. Drain the baked beans, then spread them on the bananas. Mash the beans into the bananas with a fork. Top sandwiches with remaining pieces of toast.

HINTS: *Try adding lettuce, potato chips or potato sticks to add crunch and color.*

Makes 8 servings

Grilled Anchovy and Cheese Sandwiches

Critics choice rating – 4

This sandwich is salty salty salty! The smell and texture are both really strong.

8 slices of white bread
4 slices of American cheese
1 can anchovies, drained
3 tbsp. margarine or butter

Melt 1 tbsp. butter in a frying pan on medium heat. Place 4 slices of bread in the pan. Top each bread with a slice of American cheese, then top with anchovies. Butter the remaining 4 slices of bread on one side, then close each sandwich with the butter side up. Fry until the cheese has begun to melt, then flip the sandwiches and fry on the other side until golden brown. Serve immediately.

HINTS: *Serve with potato chips or anything that is salty. Spread the first slice of bread with tomato sauce for a pizzalike sandwich with a bony twist.*

Makes 4 servings

Uptight Hamburgers

Critics choice rating – 1

The secret to this recipe is to pack the hamburger patties as tightly as you can. The tighter you pack the hamburger the harder and more miserable they will become when cooked. The juice doesn't have a chance to marinate the burger, making it very uptight. Although you may be tempted, do not—I repeat, DO NOT—add anything—no seasoning or bread crumbs, not even salt and pepper—to the beef.

1 lb. ground beef

Several hours before cooking, pound the ground beef into patties. Place them in the coldest part of the freezer for several hours. Without thawing, place the frozen patties on a hot barbecue or into a hot frying pan and cook until well done.

HINTS: *Be sure you really pack the patties tightly by hand or with a mold. It takes a strong person to pack the meat as tightly as needed for this recipe. Be sure the meat is cooked thoroughly.*

Makes 2-4 servings

Peanut Butter Chicken Nugget Goo

Critics choice rating – 1 Microwave dish

This dish is a fast-food nightmare. You can serve the peanut butter as a dipping sauce, but most people don't heat peanut butter, so they are really repulsed. Some children may actually like this dish since it combines their favorite foods. Their delight will probably make the adults you are serving even more skeptical about its edibility.

1 package frozen breaded chicken nuggets
2 oz. peanut butter
1 cup cold water

Cook the chicken nuggets according to the microwave directions given on the box. Melt the peanut butter in the microwave, then immediately mix in the cold water. The mixture will be lumpy and greasy. Mix the chicken and the peanut butter sauce together and serve.

HINTS: *Be sure that you cover the dish in which you heat the peanut butter with wax paper when melting, or it can explode in the microwave and create quite a mess. Also be sure that the sauce is not too hot when you serve it, since peanut butter can stick to the roof of your mouth and cause burns.*

Makes 4 servings

Cold Bean and Butter Sandwiches

Critics choice rating – 2

The Miserable Meal version of Beans on Toast.

1 can baked beans
2 tbsp. softened butter or margarine
8 slices bread

Butter the bread and layer on the beans straight from the can. Smear the beans into the butter, then top with the other piece of bread.

HINTS: *Be sure that the beans are cold. If you heat the beans it is more like a baked bean sandwich. The beans need to be cold and greasy.*

Makes 4 servings

Yogurt Crouton Surprise Sandwiches

Critics choice rating - 5

The crunch of the croutons and carrots will remind your guests of a salad sandwich, which is in contrast with the sweetness of the yogurt. Their taste buds will be very confused.

1 carrot
1 cup strawberry yogurt
1 cup croutons
16 pieces white bread

Using a carrot peeler, sliver the carrot into thin strips. Set aside. In a small bowl, mix the yogurt and the croutons, then fold in the carrots. Spread on bread and serve.

HINTS: *Serve these sandwiches right away so the croutons and bread do not get soggy. You can also make this with ice cream and serve as a dessert.*

SERVING SUGGESTIONS: This is best served with day-old, cut-up fruit as a garnish.

Makes 8 servings

Dinner

Marinated Flank Steak a la Shoe Leather

Critics choice rating – 4

Flank steak cooked this way is tough, stringy, and very salty. Your guests will think they are eating your old shoes for dinner. Serve with dull silverware or on paper plates with plastic folks and knives.

2 lb. flank steak
1 bottle soy sauce
1 pkg. bread cube stuffing

Pour the entire bottle of soy sauce over the flank steak and marinate for at least 1 hour. Preheat oven to 350 degrees. Cut a pocket in the flank steak and stuff the dry bread cubes in the pocket. Place the steak in a baking dish and bake for 1 hour or until the outside of the steak looks leathery. Do not baste the steak while it is cooking.

HINTS: *This recipe can also be prepared without the pocket stuffing. Broil the meat to enhance its stringy appearance.*

Makes 4-6 servings

Deep Fried Liver Strips

Critics choice –3

These crunchy strips are a great finger food as an appetizer, or serve them chilled with 3 Bean Salad—Baked, Pinto and String (see page 113).

- 1 lb. frozen liver
- ¼ cup milk
- 2 eggs
- 1 cup bread crumbs
- 1 cup olive oil

Cut the frozen liver into strips. In a small bowl and using a fork, mix together the eggs and milk. Dip the strips in the egg mixture, then dredge them in the bread crumbs. In a frying pan over medium heat, heat the olive oil, then fry the strips until brown and crunchy.

HINTS: *Liver strips can be served hot or cold. It doesn't seem to matter, since people can't figure out the combination. The smell is the only give away, so cook these ahead of time and air out your house before your guests arrive.*

Makes 10-12 servings

Lava Rock Meatballs and Spaghetti Lunar Landing

Critics choice rating – 3

This recipe is my personal favorite. The crunch of the meatballs is a real crowd stopper.

1 lb. frozen ground beef, not lean
Dash garlic salt
1 lb. green spaghetti noodles
1 jar spaghetti sauce, not chunky
1 small can water chestnuts
1 package frozen pea pods

FOR THE LAVA ROCK MEATBALLS: Defrost the meat in the microwave. Roll the meat into 1-inch balls. Place the balls in a frying pan, then take a spatula and press them into a triangular shape. Sprinkle with garlic salt. Fry on high, turning as each side gets until very crispy and they look like triangular lunar rock specimens, approximately 5 minutes per side.

FOR THE SPAGHETTI LUNAR LANDING: Cook the spaghetti in boiling water for 20 minutes. Drain. Mix the sauce with the cooked spaghetti. Add drained water chestnuts, frozen pea pods, and mix. Top with the lava rocks and serve.

HINTS: *Do not pour any sauce over the meatballs. They should look as dry as lava rocks.*

Make 6 servings

Lumpy Gray Surprise Balls

Critics choice rating – 5 Microwave recipe

This recipe was designed to attack the sense of "does this look good?" The color is wrong, the shape is weird, and the taste is bad, unless you are serving it to someone who just loves onions. Then you will have to hope that they hate the dishes you serve with these lumpy surprises.

2 lb. ground beef
½ cup bread crumbs
2 eggs
8 small onions
½ cup oil

Mix the beef, bread crumbs, and eggs together until gooey in texture. Peel the onions and trim off the top and bottom. With your fingers, roll the meat around the onion. Place the meatballs in a microwave-safe dish and cover with waxed paper. Cook on high in the microwave for 15 to 20 minutes, turning the meatballs once at 10 minutes. Adjust the cooking time if the onions begin to explode in the microwave.

HINTS: *This recipe is only effective if you use a microwave. The meat turns an ugly ashen color. Be sure to use onions that are no more that 1" to 1-½" in diameter. Pearl cocktail onions may be substituted. Parboil the raw onions if you would like to cut down on the cooking time.*

Makes 6 servings

Whipped Cream Chimichangas

Critics choice rating – 2

What a surprise your guests will get when they realize that the sour cream on these chimis is not what they expect!

1 box frozen chimichangas
1 tub frozen nondairy whipped topping or whipped cream
1 cup shredded lettuce
5 oz. Colby cheese, grated

Prepare the chimichangas using the microwave directions on the package. Top with a dollop of whipped topping, a sprinkle of shredded lettuce and cheese.

HINTS: *Try whipped butter or margarine instead of whipped topping. If you plan to use whipped butter, the chimis should be cool to the touch.*

Makes 6 servings

Onion Chili Bricks

Critics choice rating – 4

This dish looks just terrible. The red of the chili powder contrasts with the white of the onion, producing a real stomach turner. There is an added surprise in the miserable taste combination of chili powder, meat loaf, and semi-raw onions. Enjoy!

2 lb. ground beef
2 eggs
½ cup chili powder or ¼ cup chili oil
8 small onions

Preheat oven to 400 degrees. Mix the beef, chili powder, and eggs together until gooey in texture. Peel the onions and trim the top and bottom. Leaving them whole, mix them into the beef mixture. Place the mixture in a loaf pan, making sure the onions are evenly distributed. Bake at 400 degrees for 80 minutes. Serve warm.

HINTS: *Slice the onion chili brick as you would meat loaf. Since the onions are not completely cooked you will reveal an interesting variety of textures in the slices.*

Makes 6 servings

Chunky Beef Fruit Stew

Critics choice rating – 2

Since the beef in this dish is not browned first it has a very gray and grainy look and taste to it. The cooked fruit will be brown on the edges. Your guests will take one look and say, "Oh, this is different."

- 2 lbs. stew beef
- 1 can beef broth
- 2 cups water
- 3 apples
- 1 medium cantaloupe
- 1 lb. seedless grapes

Preheat the oven to 375 degrees. Place the beef in a baking pan. Cover with the broth and one cup of the water. Cover the baking pan and cook for 45 to 50 minutes, until the meat is falling apart. Core, but do not peel, the apples. Cut them into cubes. Cut the cantaloupe into cubes. Use whole grapes. Add the fruit and the remaining water and cook an additional 20 minutes, uncovered. Serve hot.

HINTS: *Use any combination of fruits that you like. Citrus, such as lemon or grapefruit, will add tartness. However these fruits may prevent your other fruits from turning brown. Pineapple will add sweetness and texture, especially if it is overcooked and becomes stringy and chewy.*

SERVING SUGGESTIONS: This dish is very thin and watery so it is especially awful when served over potatoes or pasta.

Makes 8 servings

Chicken Pot Food

Critics choice rating – 2

The combination of the chicken and the chili is actually good tasting. The large amount of liquid and the spinach usually makes the dish thin and soupy and the crust soggy. It loses its home baked pie look very early in the process.

3 boneless chicken breasts
1 can chili and beans
1 jar of chicken gravy
1 can spinach
½ cup roasted nuts
1 can beef broth
1 pie shell with topper

Broil the chicken breasts on each side until cooked, approximately 20 minutes. Set aside to cool. Preheat oven to 425 degrees. In a separate bowl, mix the chili and beans, chicken gravy, drained spinach, nuts, and broth. Cube the chicken and add to the chili mixture. Pour mixture into the pie shell and top and vent the pie. Bake for 30 minutes or until top crust turns brown. Serve hot.

HINTS: *Any combination of foods that are not normally in a pot pie makes for an interesting arrangement. Try crackers, candies, fruit, or canned or potted meats for a variation.*

Makes 4 servings

Dessert

Coconut Ice with Whole Kernel Corn

Critics choice rating – 2

Use this recipe in mixed-up course dining to really throw your guests off. Sometimes they think it is some sort of sorbet refresher, so they are more apt to try it. The beauty of this dish is that your family and guests eyes can accept the way it looks, but it is the taste combination that will send them running to the nearest restaurant.

2 cups of crushed ice
1 cup whole kernel frozen corn
½ cup grated coconut

Place the crushed ice in a bowl and mix in the corn. Add ¼ cup coconut and mix again. Scoop up the mixture and form it into round balls in pudding cups. Place the cups in the freezer for ½ hour or until ready to serve. Top with the remaining coconut and serve.

HINTS: *You can use frozen peas instead of frozen corn.*

SERVING SUGGESTIONS: Try different toppings or syrups for an added twist. Salt is also good since it melts the ice, just as on your sidewalk on an icy day.

Makes 4 servings

Cherry Tomato Chocolate Cake

Critics choice rating – 4

This cake fools the eye and then the taste buds. At first glance, your guests will think the tomatoes must be cherries. When they take a bite and find that the frosting is not sweet they may get a sign that they can't judge this cake by its frosting.

1 package chocolate cake mix
1 pint cherry tomatoes
1 tub sour cream

Prepare the cake mix as directed, except mix in half of the whole cherry tomatoes. Bake the cake in two pans as for a layer cake. Cut the remaining cherry tomatoes into thin slices. Place the sliced cherry tomatoes between the two cake layers. Frost the cake with sour cream.

HINTS: *Use real canned frosting if you do not want to reveal the surprise filling until they bite in. Yogurt can also be used for frosting.*

Makes 10 servings

Onion Ice Cream with Gravy Topping

Critics choice rating – 5

This recipe sends most guests heading for the hills. The smell of ice cream mixed with onions is just indescribable. The texture won't be believed.

1 whole yellow onion
1 quart vanilla ice cream, softened
1 jar brown gravy

Chop the onion into fine mince. Set 1/3 cup onion aside and hand mix the remaining onion into the softened ice cream. Place the ice cream in the freezer to harden. Place one scoop of ice cream in a bowl and top with the cold brown gravy. Sprinkle with the reserved onion mince.

HINTS: *Use red peppers or scallions instead of onion. Cold tomato sauce can be used as a substitute for the gravy.*

Makes 8-100 servings
(since nobody will eat this recipe anyway)

Munchie Crunchy Brownie Goo

Critics choice rating – 4

- 1 box brownie mix
- 1 cup oil
- 1 cup chocolate-flavored cereal

Preheat oven to temperature specified on the brownie mix box. Follow the directions on the brownie mix box, then add an additional cup of oil and the cereal. Bake as directed, but shorten the baking time by 10 minutes.

HINTS: *Other things that can be added to give the brownies additional goo and crunch: peanut butter, syrup, caramel, marshmallows, potato or taco chips. Do not overcook. This recipe is meant to be gooey. It is the undercooking that creates the desired effect.*

Makes a 9 x 12 pan of brownies

Oookie Cookies

Critics choice rating – 3

1 tube oatmeal slice-and-bake cookies
½ cup frozen corn
½ cup frozen peas

Preheat oven to temperature specified on the package. Place the cookie mix in a bowl. Add the corn and peas and mix well. Form the cookie mix into balls and place on a cookie tray. Follow the baking directions on the cookie wrapper.

HINTS: *Other things that can be added to give the cookies additional "oookie": cooked pasta, beans, rice. These cookies burn easily on the bottom. An underdone cookie is acceptable for this recipe.*

Makes 2 dozen cookies

Ice Cream Tacos

Critics choice rating – 4

6 taco shells
1 quart ice cream – any flavor
½ cup grated cheese
½ cup shredded lettuce
½ cup green onion
1 cup picante sauce

Make three small scoops of ice cream and carefully place them into the taco shell. Pour a small amount of picante over the ice cream and top with a layer of shredded lettuce, a layer of green onion and a layer of grated cheese. Top the ice cream taco with an additional layer of picante sauce.

Hints: *Refried beans or cherries can be added to the toppings on the taco. The ice cream can be mixed with green chilies, taco chips, or rice. Sprinkles, fruit toppings or nuts can also be added to the taco for a Miserable Meal classic.*

Makes 6 tacos

Side Dishes

Pineapple Gelatin Mold

Critics choice – 1

Why do gelatin boxes always say that you shouldn't add pineapple? Because the manufacturers of gelatin want you to keep buying their product, which you won't do if you make a miserable meal recipe with it. With this recipe, you will discover that pineapple reacts with gelatin so that it will not set up, no matter how long you leave it in the refrigerator. All it will make is a miserable mess. Those brave enough to try it will realize that it actually tastes very good. It just looks so bad that they won't even want to try it.

- 1 package of diet cherry gelatin
- 1 small can of drained pineapple chunks

Follow the directions on the gelatin box. Add the pineapple as you would any other canned fruit. Place in the fridge to chill.

SERVING SUGGESTIONS: *Serve this as a side dish in a cup, it is too runny to be put on a plate.*

Makes 6 servings

Jalapeño Gelatin Squares

Critics choice – 5

The taste of this is initially sweet with a kick that will make most people stand up and yell, "Yee-ha!" The clear gelatin does allow your guests a peak at what is to come. There are some people who really like hot and very spicy. Know your guests, because this can be a real surprise for the taste buds. Some do love it, most hate it, but in all cases this dish is remembered.

1 package lime gelatin
1 small jar jalapeño peppers, drained

Follow the directions on the gelatin. Add the jalapeños as you would add any other canned fruit. Chill as directed.

Makes 6-8 servings

Hot Fudge French Fries

Critics choice – 2 Microwave recipe

1 package frozen french fries
1 pinch salt to taste
1 jar microwave hot fudge sauce

Heat the french fries in the microwave until hot, usually 6 to 8 minutes. They should not be brown, but should look white and pasty. Shake salt onto the french fries. Heat the hot fudge sauce in the microwave as directed. Pour the sauce over the french fries, as you would a dipping sauce or catsup.

HINTS: *Try mashed potatoes or cooked pasta instead of french fries.*

SERVING SUGGESTIONS: Serve this recipe in ice cream dishes. It's a hot fudge sundae with a potato surprise.

Makes 6-8 servings

Crunch and Bite Mashed Potatoes

Critics choice – 5

This dish has an all-white theme. The finer you chop the mix-ins, the more of a surprise they will be.

- 1 cup instant mashed potato mix
- 1 can water chestnuts, drained
- 1 medium onion, cubed
- 2 tablespoons white horseradish
- 4 radishes, peeled and finely chopped

Follow the directions on the mashed potato box. When they are done, mix in the water chestnuts, onion, horseradish, and radishes. Mix well and serve.

HINTS: *This bites and crunches from the very first spoonful. Keeping the recipe all in white is very important for the surprise element. You can also reserve some plain mashed potatoes to frost the top of the dish and prevent your guests from guessing the surprise.*

Makes 6-8 servings

Barbecued Pasta

Critics choice – 3

Most people have never had barbecued pasta, so their reaction is immediate. For best effect, wait to cook the noodles until they are all standing around. Watch their mouths drop open when you put noodles on the grill.

3 cups water
3 tbsp. olive oil
1 package lasagna noodles
1 jar barbecue sauce

Bring the water to a boil. Add the olive oil and pasta and cook the noodles until they begin to soften, approximately 5 minutes in boiling water. Drain noodles and place flat on a plate to cool. Heat the grill to high. With a brush, spread barbecue sauce on both sides of the noodles. Place the noodles on the grill until there are grill marks on the noodles, approximately 1 minute. Turn the noodles and cook the other side for approximately 1 minute.

HINTS: *Have a big scraper ready in case the noodles begin to crumble. (This dish can also be served as scrapings.) Another option is to just burn the edges of the noodles so they have a real camp fire flavor.*

Makes 6-8 servings

Veggie Dredgie Mooch

Critics choice – 2

This dish smells interesting, to say the least. Take note of what your guests smell first. Some smell the liver while others notice the marshmallows. Either way, once they see the combination they usually leave this dish alone.

- 1 pkg. frozen vegetables, such as Italian or Chinese
- 1 cup marshmallows
- 1 can liver pate
- 1 can frozen lemonade

Preheat oven to 400 degrees. Place the frozen vegetables in a large baking pan. Add the liver pate and the marshmallows and mix well until the mixture is brownish in color. Pour the undiluted lemonade over the mixture and bake for 20 minutes.

HINTS: *Be sure not to thaw the vegetables. Do not dilute the lemonade, use it straight from the can.*

Makes 4-6 servings

Salads and Soups

Pea Gelatin Salad

Critics choice rating – 3

- 1 can peas or 1 pkg. frozen peas
- 1 pkg. sugar free cherry or white gelatin
- 1 bunch parsley

Follow the directions on the box to make the gelatin. Chill and cut into cubes in different shapes and sizes. Drain the peas if using canned, or use frozen peas straight from the package. Toss them with gelatin. Top with the parsley.

HINTS: *The peas have to be cool or cold, or they will melt the gelatin and creates a sauce. You may substitute whole kernel corn or spinach for the peas.*

Makes 8 servings

Beet Soup Fizz

Critics choice rating – 3

- 1 can beets
- 1 bottle ginger ale
- 1 box croutons

Mix the beets with their liquid with the ginger ale. Top with croutons.

Serve immediately.

HINTS: *The beets will make this soup red or pink, depending on how much ginger ale you add. You may want to add some food coloring to preserve its natural red color.*

SERVING SUGGESTIONS: The sooner you serve this soup the fizzier it will be. It was created as a cold soup, but I have found that it is equally miserable served hot. Top the cold version with a dollop of sour cream, and float lemon slices in the hot version. When your family and guests get tired of this soup, surprise them by serving it as dessert. Another creative way to use it is to make ice cubes to complement their favorite drinks.

Makes 8 servings

Hot Pea Soup Dressing Salad

Critics choice rating – 1

1 can split pea soup
1 head romaine lettuce
1 medium tomato

Tear the lettuce into chunks and place in a salad bowl. Chill the salad in the refrigerator. While the salad is chilling, open the can of pea soup and heat as directed on the can. Cut the tomato into pieces of several different shapes and sizes and set aside. Sprinkle the tomato pieces on the greens, then pour the hot pea soup over the salad and serve.

HINTS: *Keep the pea soup thick so that it globs on the salad and does not run to the bottom of the salad bowl.*

SERVING SUGGESTIONS: This delectable dressing can also be used as a thick and hearty topping for eggs, meats and poultry. Or chill the cooked soup for a more coarsely textured sauce. It is also interesting to serve this dressing in both its hot and cold versions on the same salad or dish. The pea soup also freezes well and can be used as a miserable substitution for ice cubes in drinks.

Makes 8 servings

Pickle Peach Slaw

Critics choice rating – 5

This dish looks really bad, but the taste is actually passable. It's the texture, though—the crunch of the pickles with the mush of the peaches—that gets them every time.

1 pkg. shredded cabbage
1 jar cold pack sour pickles, sandwich sliced
1 can sliced peaches
½ cup oil

Place the shredded cabbage in a large mixing bowl. Drain the pickle juice and the peach juice and set aside. Mix the pickles and peaches into the shredded cabbage. In a separate bowl, mix together the oil, pickle juice and peach juice. Pour the dressing over the salad and toss until cabbage is well coated.

HINTS: *Try fruit cocktail or any canned fruit with a syrup sauce for a little variety. You can also use root beer instead of oil for a fizzy, tangy taste.*

SERVING SUGGESTION: This slaw is very sweet and very sour. It is best to serve it with something salty.

Makes 8-12 servings

3 Bean Salad–Baked, Pinto and String

Critics choice rating – 3

A miserable version of an old-time classic.

1 can Boston-style baked beans
1 can cooked pinto beans
1 can green string beans

Drain each of the cans and set the liquid aside. In a bowl, add the baked beans, pinto beans and string beans, and toss lightly. Mix the liquids together and use as the dressing to be passed with the salad.

HINTS: *Do not overmix the salad, but let each bean show through. If you overmix, the salad will look like brown mud. Once the salad is prepared, place it in the refrigerator for about an hour so that the flavors have a chance to mingle and mature, and to keep the beans firm.*

Makes 10-12 servings

Sort of Fresh Fruit Salad

Critics choice – I

I selected the fruits in this salad because when they are peeled and cut up they turn brown far faster than any other fruits. For this to be a Miserable Meal recipe, force yourself not to use lemon or citrus juice to keep fruit from turning color. This fruit salad is meant to look brown and wilted.

2 large apples
2 medium pears
4 bananas

Peel and cube the fruits, keeping them separate. Let them sit out in the open air for a half hour. Mix them together in a large bowl and set mix out again for 20 minutes. Place mix in the refrigerator overnight. Serve the next day.

SERVING SUGGESTIONS: This recipe is appropriate for any meal. In fact, make enough for every meal. The more meals you serve with it, the older it looks. Complement this dish with other aged foods, such as wilted lettuce or dried sprouts. Dry your sprouts by spreading them on a cooking sheet and placing them in a 450 degree over for 10 minutes.

Makes 8-10 servings

Birthday Cake Salad

Critics choice rating – 3

This dish is salad and dessert all in one.

It is an especially easy salad because it doesn't need a dressing. The frosting from the cake takes care of that.

1 store-bought frosted birthday cake
1 head lettuce
1 pkg. cherry tomatoes

Cut the cake into 2-inch squares, and set aside. Tear the lettuce and place it in a large salad bowl. Add cherry tomatoes and mix well. Carefully fold in the squares and serve.

HINTS: *Try not to mash the cake so that it cannot be identified as cake and frosting. Freezing the cake will make it easier to cut it into squares.*

Makes 6-10 servings

Cookie Cobb Soup

Critics choice rating – 4

This soup looks like old cereal with a corn cob in the center.

2 cans chicken broth
1 pkg. frozen corn-on-the-cob
2 cups water
1 box cookies

Pour the chicken broth into a large pot. Cut the frozen ears of corn in half and place them in the pot. Add the water to the pot. Boil the corn for 15 minutes. During the last 5 minutes of boiling, add half of the cookies. Mix. Pour the soup into bowls, with at least one cob per bowl, and make a top crust with the remaining cookies.

HINTS: *Add the top cookies just before you serve the soup. I prefer the bite-sized chocolate chip or oatmeal cookies. Substitute a can of clam chowder for one of the cups of water. It will give the soup a milkier and chunkier look and texture.*

Makes 6-8 servings

Turkey Yam Soup

Critics choice rating – 3

This dish is very orange and thick. The taste is not too bad; it's the look that will get them.

2 cans yams in syrup
3 cups water
1 lb. cubed cooked turkey breast

In a pot, mix the yams with syrup with the water and boil for 10 minutes. Cut the turkey into cubes and place in the pot and boil for 45 minutes. Serve immediately.

SERVING SUGGESTIONS: For a fall look, accent this dish with things that are green and brown—such as avocado and raisins—for a fall look. In winter, add marshmallows to the top of each bowl. This will make the soup very sweet.

Makes 6-8 servings

Ice Cream Stroganoff Soup

Critics choice rating – 2

The secret to this dish is that it confuses the palate because it is cold and hot at the same time. The soup will be different colors depending on the kind of ice cream you use. The first taste will be creamy, so it will take your guests a few bites to realize that they are eating warm ice cream mixed with meat.

½ lb. chuck steak
1 onion
2 cups cubed carrots
1 half gallon ice cream, any flavor
1 pkg. chocolate sprinkles

Slice the meat into strips and place in a pot and cook on medium high heat until browned. Mix in the onions and carrots and cook until soft. Take off heat and place the meat and vegetables in a soup bowl. Add the ice cream on top, but do not mix. Spread the sprinkles over the top. Serve immediately.

HINTS: *Once you put the ice cream on top of the meat, do not mix it. Let the heat of the meat melt the ice cream. This will give the soup a lumpy look and make pockets of hot and cold.*

Makes 6-8 servings

Miscellaneous

Cinnamon Liver Spread

Critics choice rating – 2

The smell and taste of this dish will make your guests wonder why they ever agreed to come to your house for dinner.

1 onion
3 stalks celery
2 tbsp. oil
1 small jar ground cinnamon
1 can liver paté

Cut the onion and celery into chunks. In a frying pan over medium heat, fry the onions and celery in the oil until limp, approximately 20 minutes. Let cool. Heat the liver pate in a saucepan over medium heat until hot and bubbly. Mix the liver with the onions and celery. Add all of the cinnamon and mix well.

HINTS: *A food processor makes it easier to put this dish together, but it also makes it smoother. I prefer the chunk version for effect.*

Makes 6-10 servings

Beer with Ice

Critics choice rating – 2

Warm beer is a big social no-no, as is serving beer with ice cubes in it. Serve this refreshment on a hot summer day to guests who insist on watching sports at your house. For really pesky guests, heat the beer in the microwave.

6 pack of beer, at room temperature
1 tray ice cubes

Pour the beer into warm mugs. Add ice and serve.

HINTS: *If you do decide to heat the beer, pour it into a microwave-safe container and heat on high for 50 seconds. Tell your guests that the beer is warm, but you would be happy to add ice if they would like. Most beer drinkers will be appalled and will head for the nearest sports bar.*

Makes 6 servings

Toothpaste Canapés

Critics choice rating – 5

- 1 box crackers
- 1 tube cake decorating white frosting
- 1 tube cake decorating blue frosting

Place the crackers on a tray. Squeeze a small dab of the frosting on the crackers using a circular motion. Alternate colors so there are equal amounts of white and blue.

HINTS: *A word of caution—do not use real toothpaste in this recipe. Multi-colored frosting can add a festive twist. I particularly like the frosting with sparkles.*

SERVING SUGGESTIONS: Serve these as an appetizer for a dinner party or brunch. Be sure to announce that they are your specialty "toothpaste canapés."

Makes 15-30 servings

Oriental Freeze-Dried O-oo

Critics choice rating – 5

To some tastes, freeze-dried oriental foods are enough to make them run for the hills. Go to an oriental grocery store and select your own array of freeze-dried delicacies. They come in many varieties, including fish, vegetable, and other choices to suit any miserable meal palate.

3 packages oriental freeze dried treats

Follow the directions on the package for unfreeze-drying the contents. If you cannot read the directions because they are in a foreign language, it says, "Take a warm bowl of water, place the stuff in the bowl and let sit for 15-20 minutes."

SERVING SUGGESTIONS: Place on crackers on a tray. Serve as appetizers or as a main meal. Or consider putting them out dry in a bowl for a chiplike snack. Size up your guests before serving them this way, though. Some people actually like the stuff very much, so know your guests.

Makes 8-20 servings

Notes About the Author

Karen Kallet is a successful author, speaker, entrepreneur, and business executive. Her accomplishments in marketing and advertising include heading the advertising department for a major airline, graphic design management for a large financial institution, and media management for a national convenience store chain. She was also head of marketing for in-flight catalogs found on most airlines. She has written articles for professional publications and newspapers throughout her twenty-year career.

Kallet has now started a new career as an author and publisher, with her first accomplishment this humorous cookbook. Karen first started writing this cookbook over ten years ago and has tweaked and added to it during breaks in her career. People were always coming over to eat and chat, but Karen found she didn't enjoy the cooking, just the company. Thus, The Art of Miserable Meal Making was born. She is no longer expected to cook for, truly, when she cooks, they run.

Index

When I Cook, They Run
Book Order Form

To order this book, please fill in the information requested and send a check or money order made payable to: **Twenty12 Publishing.**

$14.95 per book plus shipping. US Dollars Only.
Call regarding volume discounts.

Sales Tax: Please add 7.15% for books shipped to Arizona addresses.
Shipping: * $4.00 for the first book and $2.00 for each additional book.
Payment: ____ Check or Money order Sorry no COD's.

_____	**When I Cook, They Run cookbooks at $14.95 EACH**	_______
	Shipping*	_______
	Arizona residents add sales tax	_______
	TOTAL	_______

Ship to:

Name____

Company______________________________________

Address______________________________________

City__________________ State______ Zip ____________

Telephone (_____)_______________

Mail To:

Twenty12 Publishing
When I Cook, They Run
P.O. Box 26756
Phoenix, AZ 85068-6756, USA

Order Now!